T0061200

WACKY COMPARISONS

HOW HEAVY?

Wacky Ways to Compare Weight

By MARK WEAKLAND ILLUSTRATED BY BILL BOLTON

How heavy is a **bus**?

How heavy is a **dog**?

Are they as heavy as a **mouse** or a **frog**?

Look inside, and you will see

just how heavy things can be!

PICTURE WINDOW BOOKS
a capstone imprint

1 bulldog with a stubby tail

weighs the same as

167 hamburgers on a scale.

1 bulldog = 45 pounds (20 kilograms); 1 burger = 4.3 ounces (122 grams)

How heavy is 1 yellow bus?

It equals 4 hippos, each making a fuss.

1 bus = 12 tons (11 metric tons); 1 hippo = 2.8 tn. (2.5 t)

How much does a **triceratops** weigh?

The same as

4.2 million

gummy bears, I dare say.

How many marshmallows will a hedgehog munch to equal its weight? 120. That's a bunch!

1 hedgehog = 30 oz. (850 g); 1 marshmallow = 0.25 oz. (7.1 g)

The weight of 1 panda bear munching bamboo

equals 709 billiard balls,

colorful and new.

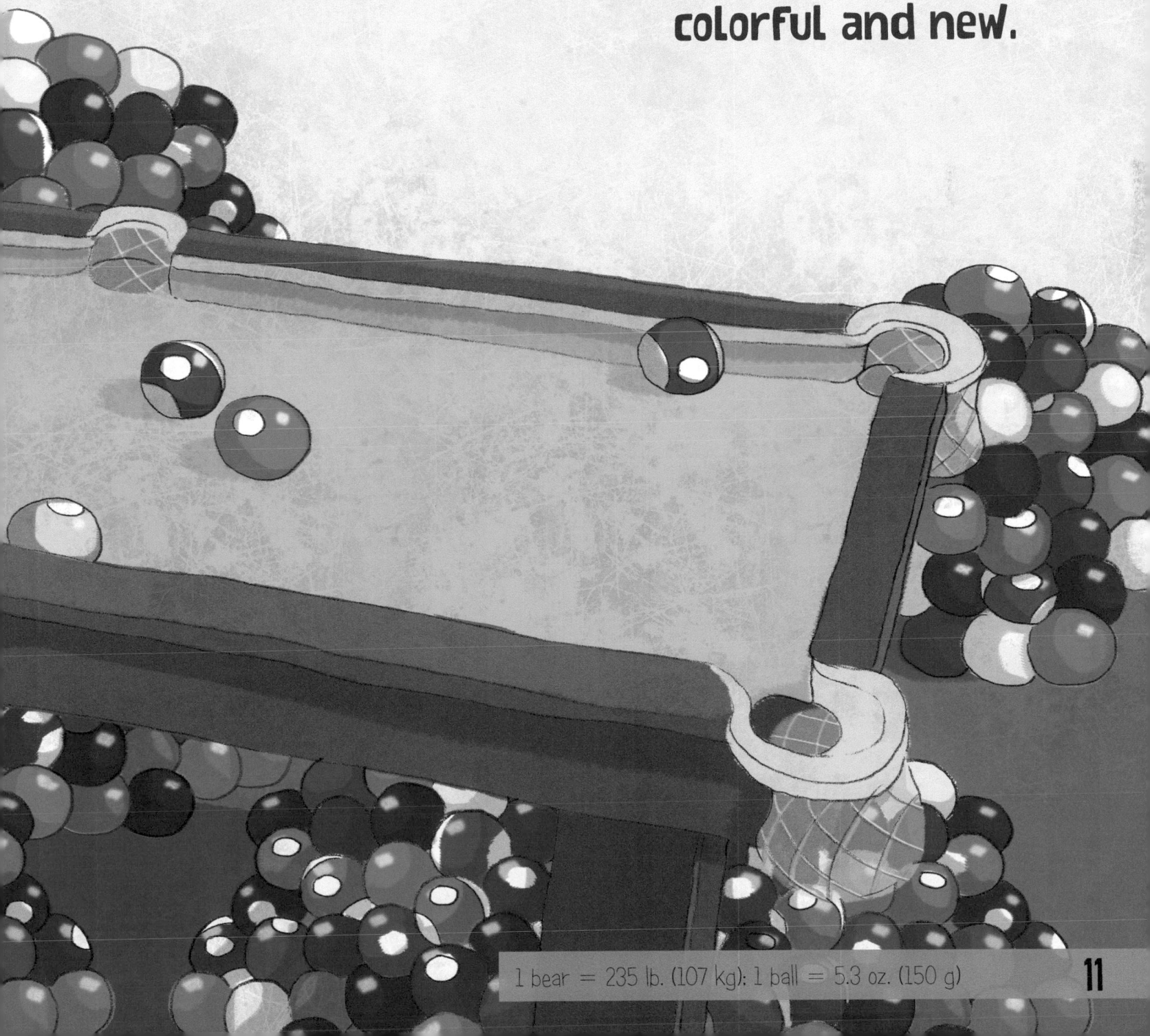

1 bear = 235 lb. (107 kg); 1 ball = 5.3 oz. (150 g)

To equal his weight, topknot to feet,
a SUMO wrestler needs
1,424 treats.

1 wrestler = 356 lb. (161 kg); 1 cupcake = 4 oz. (113 g)

1 toilet, shiny and white,

weighs nearly as much as

98 bullfrogs jumping out of sight.

1 toilet = 108 lb. (49 kg); 1 bullfrog = 1.1 lb. (499 g)

How many milk cartons
equal 1 cow?
2,222

1 cow = 1,200 lb. (544 kg); 1 carton = 0.54 lb. (245 g)

1 glowing pumpkin in need of braces

weighs the same as

7 guinea pigs making faces.

1 pumpkin = 15 lb. (6.8 kg): 1 guinea pig = 33.5 oz. (950 g)

How much does a **bulldozer** weigh?

The same as **19,000** kittens ready to play.

1 bulldozer = 19 tn. (17.2 t); 1 kitten = 2 lb. (907 g)

3.2 million mice, whisker to tail,

weigh the same as 1 big blue whale.

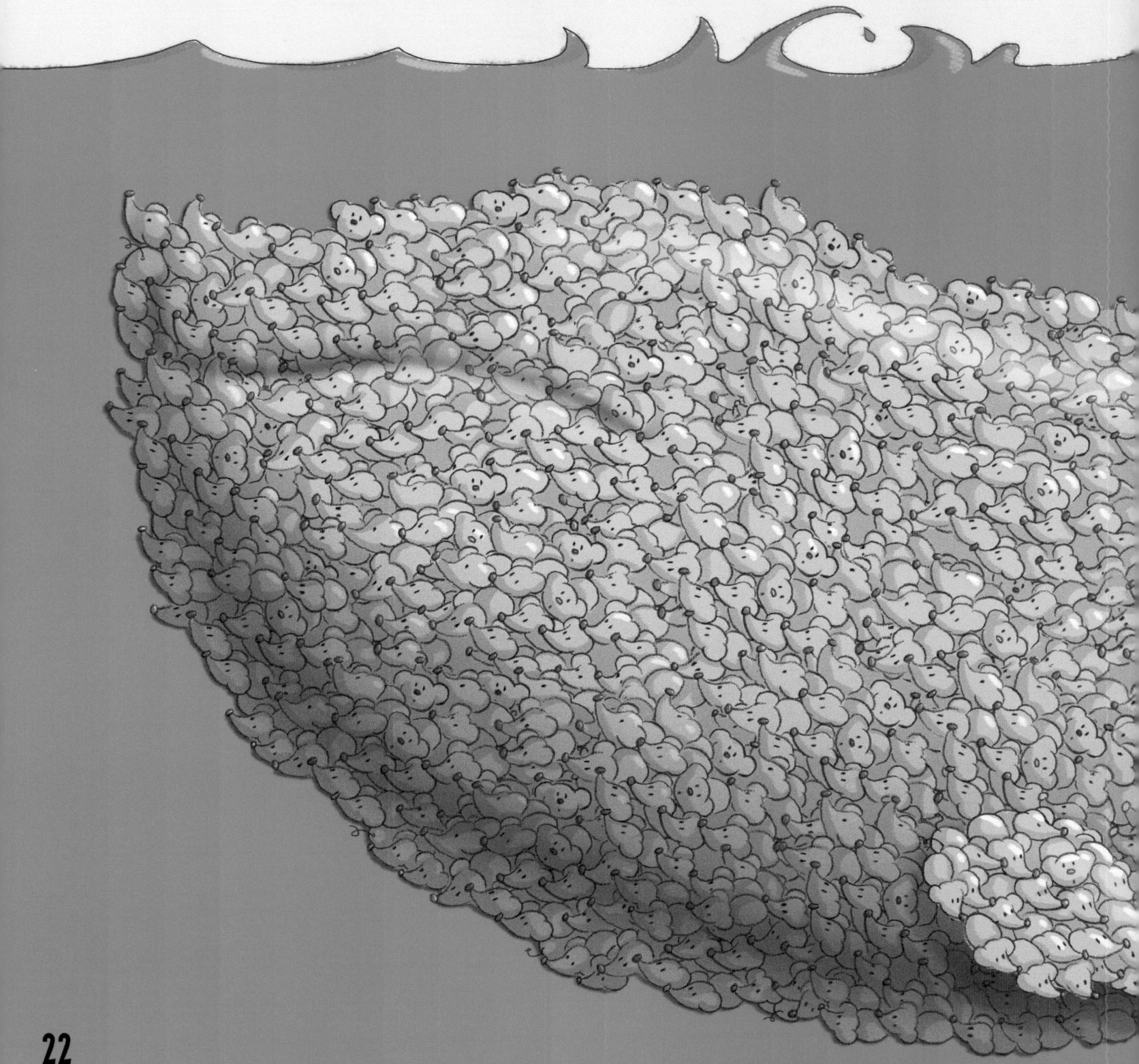

1 whale = 80 tn. (73 t); 1 mouse = 0.8 oz. (23 g)

READ MORE

Coffelt, Nancy. *Big, Bigger, Biggest!* New York: Henry Holt and Co., 2009.

Hughes, Susan. *Is It Heavy or Light?* What's the Matter? New York: Crabtree Pub. Company, 2012.

Olson, Nathan. *Heavy and Light: An Animal Opposites Book.* Animal Opposites. Mankato, Minn.: Capstone Press, 2008.

Parker, Vic. *How Heavy Is Heavy?: Comparing Vehicles.* Measuring and Comparing. Chicago: Heinemann Library, 2011.

INTERNET SITES

FactHound offers a safe, fun way to find Internet sites related to this book. All of the sites on FactHound have been researched by our staff.

Here's all you do:

Visit *www.facthound.com*

Type in this code: 9781404883222

Check out projects, games and lots more at **www.capstonekids.com**

Special thanks to our adviser, Terry Flaherty, PhD, Professor of English, Minnesota State University, Mankato, for his expertise.

Editor: Jill Kalz
Designer: Ashlee Suker
Art Director: Nathan Gassman
Production Specialist: Eric Manske
The illustrations in this book were created digitally.

Picture Window Books are published by Capstone,
1710 Roe Crest Drive, North Mankato, Minnesota 56003
www.capstonepub.com

Copyright © 2014 by Picture Window Books, a Capstone imprint. All rights reserved. No part of this publication may be reproduced in whole or in part, or stored in a retrieval system, or transmitted in any form or by any means, electronic, mechanical, photocopying, recording, or otherwise, without written permission of the publisher.

Library of Congress Cataloging-in-Publication Data
Weakland, Mark.
How heavy? : wacky ways to compare weight / by Mark Weakland; illustrated by Bill Bolton.
pages cm. — (Wacky comparisons)
Summary: "Compares various heavy objects to lighter objects in unique, illustrated ways"—Provided by publisher.
Audience: K to grade 3.
Includes bibliographical references.
ISBN 978-1-4048-8322-2 (library binding)
ISBN 978-1-4795-1912-5 (paperback)
ISBN 978-1-4795-1908-8 (eBook PDF)
1. Weight (Physics)—Measurement—Juvenile literature. 2. Weight judgment—Juvenile literature. 3. Comparison (Philosophy)—Juvenile literature. I. Bolton, Bill, 1968– illustrator. II. Title.

QC106.W43 2014
530.8—dc23 2013012152

Photo Credit
Capstone/Karon Dubke, 7 (gummy bears)

LOOK FOR ALL THE BOOKS IN THE SERIES:

Printed in the United States 5961